Presented to:

_____

From:

_____

Date:

_____

You have captured my heart . . .

SONG OF SOLOMON 4:9 NLT

of Love

*Heartwarming Messages
to Say I Love You*

A DIVISION OF SIMON & SCHUSTER
New York London Toronto Sydney

Our purpose at Howard Books is to:
- *Increase faith* in the hearts of growing Christians
- *Inspire holiness* in the lives of believers
- *Instill hope* in the hearts of struggling people everywhere

Because He's coming again!

Published by Howard Books, a division of Simon & Schuster, Inc.
1230 Avenue of the Americas, New York, NY 10020
www.howardpublishing.com

Kisses of Love © 2007 by Dave Bordon & Associates, LLC

All rights reserved, including the right to reproduce this book or portions thereof in any form whatsoever. For information, address Howard Subsidiary Rights Department, 1230 Avenue of the Americas, New York, NY 10020.

ISBN: 978-1-4767-9003-9

10 9 8 7 6 5 4 3 2 1

HOWARD and colophon are registered trademarks of Simon & Schuster, Inc.

For information regarding special discounts for bulk purchases, please contact: Simon & Schuster Special Sales at 1-800-456-6798 or business@simonandschuster.com.

Project developed by Bordon Books, Tulsa, Oklahoma
Project writing and compilation by Christy Phillippe in association with Bordon Books
Edited by Chrys Howard
Cover design by Greg Jackson, Thinkpen Design

Scripture quotations marked NLT are taken from the *Holy Bible,* New Living Translation, copyright © 1996. Used by permission of Tyndale House Publishers, Inc., Wheaton, Illinois 60189. All rights reserved.

Introduction

A kiss. It's short. Sweet. And packed with love. That's what *Kisses of Love* is all about. Each page of this book is a message filled to overflowing with the love I have for you. As you read, I hope you'll experience that love, that you'll know how special you are to me, and that you'll realize how much I cherish the joy you bring to my life.

*There is only one happiness in life—
to love and to be loved.*

GEORGE SAND

I love you!

You are my favorite person
in the world—no one else even
comes close.

I love everything about you:
your sparkling eyes . . .

your tender embrace . . .

your comforting touch . . .

your smile that lights up my world.

I don't know how you do
what you do to me;
I know only that I love
how you do it!

The way you tell a joke . . .

hold me close . . .

try to eat with chopsticks . . .

grin when you're up to something . . .

spoil me rotten . . .

kiss me at the end of the day—
all these things make me love you
even more.

You bring music, melody, and meaning into my life,

and you make every day a wonderful surprise.

Your strength carries me
through the hard times,

and just when my world needs a
touch of color,

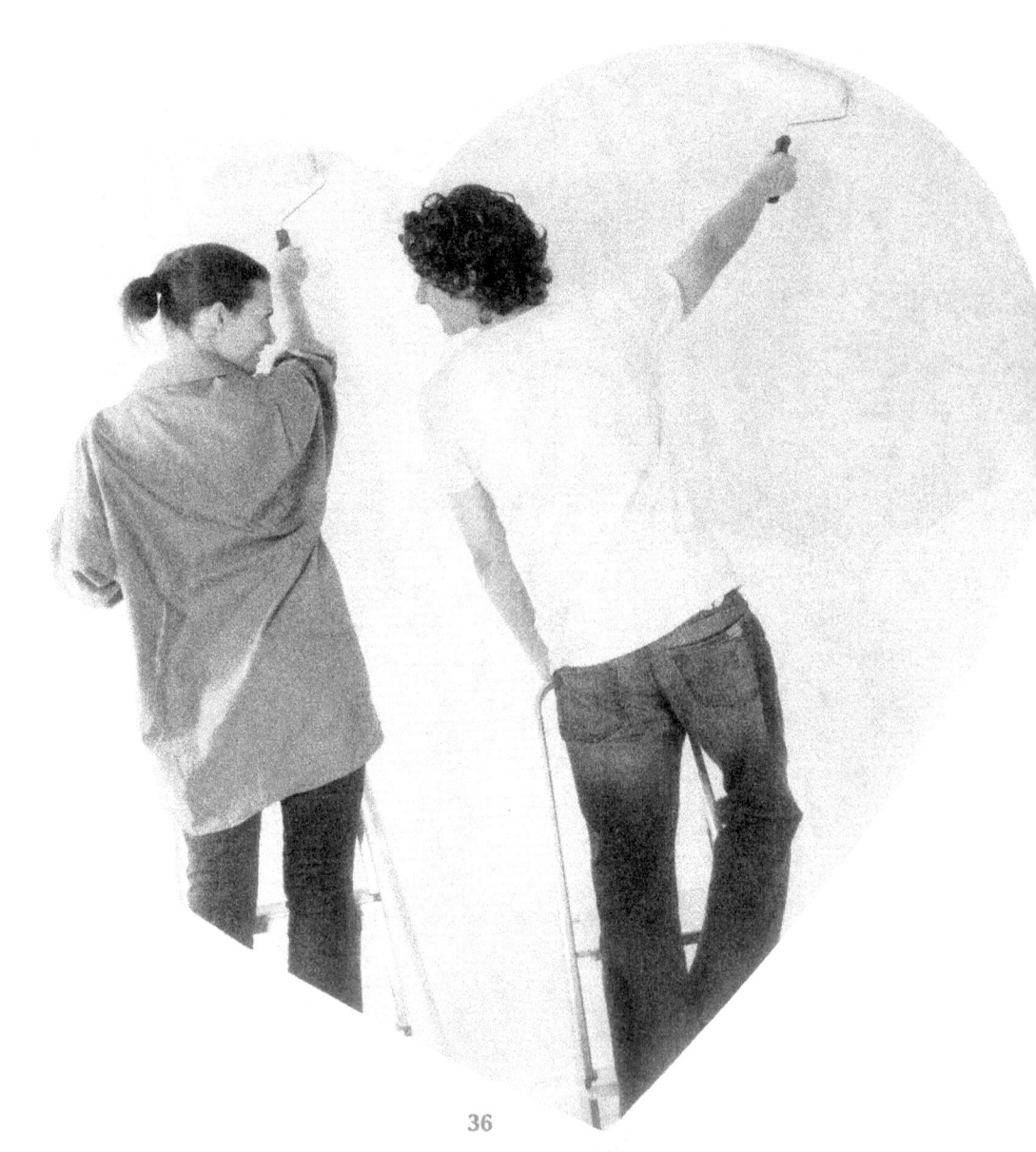

your love adds a bright new
rainbow.

With you I am safe to be myself, because you love every part of me:

my goofy side . . .

my adventurous side . . .

my prickly side . . .

my whiny side . . .

my vulnerable side . . .

and my sentimental side.

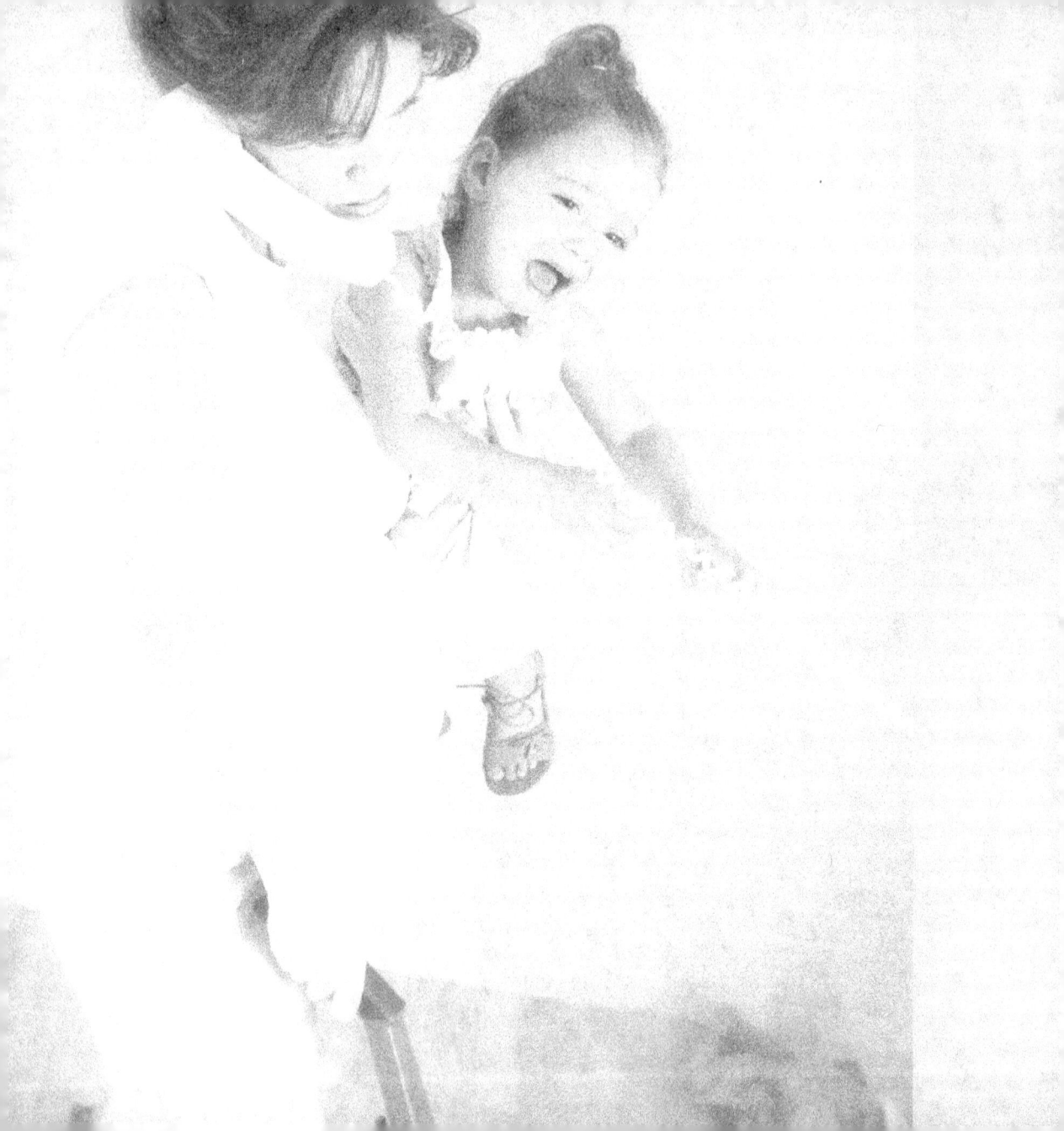

On days when I feel less than attractive,

your love makes me feel beautiful.

And on days when I am
on top of the world,

you are right there with me
to celebrate.

Your hugs make me feel warm and secure,

and your kisses make me
weak in the knees.

Life is not always sunshine and roses.

But when we hit the rough spots,

I know we can
see them through together.

Conflict makes us stronger because we meet it with mutual respect.

We may not always agree, but we listen and try to understand each other . . .

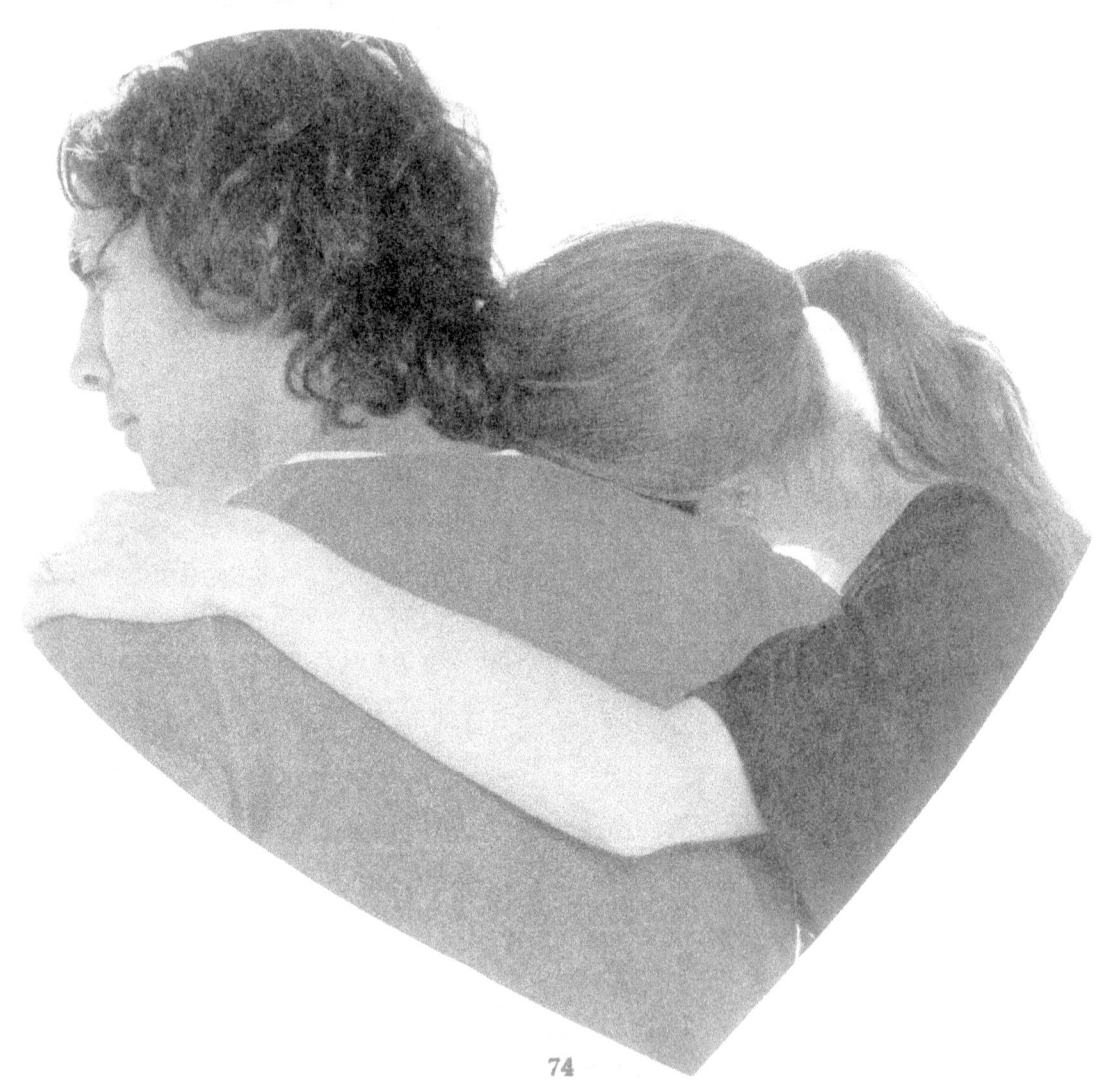

bear with and forgive each other . . .

believe the best of each other

We are a team, and
together we are strong

no matter what life brings our way—
whether *mundane* . . .

or exhilarating . . .

whether challenging...

or relaxing.

Whether wild and crazy,

or sweet and tender,

it's always better sharing it with you.

You care for me like
no one else does,

and you always remember
the little and big things: my
favorite ice cream . . .

my birthday . . .

the day we first met.

You are like homemade waffles
on a snowy day . . .

like the sun breaking through
the clouds . . .

and like the path that leads me home.

There's no other place
I'd rather be than
with you.

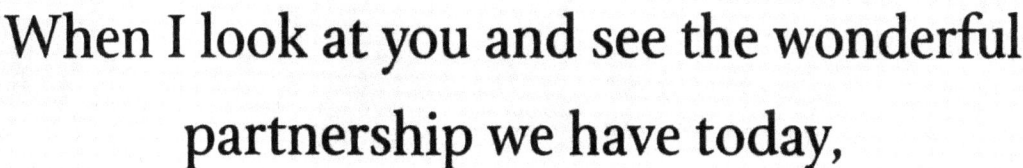

When I look at you and see the wonderful partnership we have today,

I am confident of a bright and beautiful future for us.

Your love gives me hope,

and you are my *dream* come true.

You are my one and
only true love.

I will always cherish the gift
God gave me when He gave me
you!

LOOK FOR THESE BOOKS

Kisses of Comfort

Kisses of Encouragement

Kisses from a Friend's Heart

Kisses from a Mother's Heart

Kisses from a Sister's Heart

www.ingramcontent.com/pod-product-compliance
Lightning Source LLC
Chambersburg PA
CBHW051416070526
44584CB00023B/3457